Andraste's Hair

ELEANOR REES was born in Birkenhead, Merseyside in 1978. Her pamphlet collection *Feeding Fire* received an Eric Gregory Award in 2002. She works in the community as a poet, running writing workshops for The Windows Project and also teaches in higher education. Eleanor is a member of the Word Hoard, Huddersfield and often collaborates with other writers, musicians and artists. She lives in Liverpool.

Also by Eleanor Rees

Feeding Fire (Spout Publications, 2001)

Andraste's Hair

Eleanor Rees

CAMBRIDGE

PUBLISHED BY SALT PUBLISHING
PO Box 937, Great Wilbraham, Cambridge CB21 5JX United Kingdom

First published 2007

Printed in Great Britain by Biddles Ltd, King's Lynn, Norfolk

Typeset in Swift 9.5 / 13

ISBN 978 1 84471 304 2 paperback

Salt Publishing Ltd gratefully acknowledges
the financial assistance of Arts Council England

1 3 5 7 9 8 6 4 2

Contents

Acknowledgements

'Andraste's Hair' and 'Castle Hill' were first published in *Stand*; 'Night Vision' in *Tears in the Fence*; 'July' in *Smoke*; 'Flood', 'Body' and 'Extracts from A Nocturnal Opera' in *Citizen 32: Sexuality*; 'Roadworks' and 'Parkland' in *Nerve*; 'Seams of Dust' and 'On Shore' in *Back to the Machine Gun*; an extract from 'A Red Moon' in *Mercy*. 'Night River' and an extract from 'A Nocturnal Opera' appeared on the *Verberate Live* CD 2005.

'A Nocturnal Opera' was written as a collaborative poem for performance with The Word Hoard, Huddersfield 2004/5 and first published in *The TEXT*, Winter 2006.

"Tell me something of this" was a commissioned collaborative poem initially shown on an interactive LED architectural interface at The Media Centre, Huddersfield in 2004.

Many thanks to all those who have supported, inspired and enabled the creation of these poems. Thanks to Dianne Darby, Keith Jafrate and the Word Hoard, Huddersfield for writing time and vision. Many thanks to all at The Windows Project with special thanks to Dave Ward for editorial advice, encouragement and insight. And also thanks to my friends and family for all their support along the way.

Night Vision

An open moon; burr of grass.
Last reaches of the spilt day
ending, the last
quiet pitch heard
in deep woods. Wet sod of dirt.
Scent of the sun's fire
passing field ruts and furrows,
seedlings, coiled roots, hedgerows;
flight of night-bird
turning tail into a sea breeze,
beak battened to the north.

～

Cloud—now stone in ocean in undertow—
drops from night above the city
into an unseen sea,
at edges of membrane and sinew.
Wade through sky. Perforate.
Pebbles of rain on pitted tarmac
clutter the way home;
night-splashed, corroded.

~

A cold touch in a bleeding house.
An open door. Sores.

And I dream you are the rising sun:

where are your bones, baby? Where are your bones?
    I've hurt for you — for your nights.
    Each turn and flat-packed mile
walked to catch the drift and knack of ends
    and fugitive ends.
Back alleys of the city burn.
Night boils outside the window.
The streets smoulder as morning comes.

Roadworks

1.

Sometime around midday.

The tarmac is biting at my ankles.
Well-lit sky snaps fast and short
as the street opens up to tumble
me into an underground
of corpses and snowdrift
and horses with gold faces
and pretty girls with bees in their hair
and silverfish with steel legs
and smiling boys with tattooed penises
and wet hearts in jars like flowers or flames
and invisible ledges of air
and rock face of baby's faces
and heavy tongues loll like dogs
and tall ships crash on cavern walls
and underground rivers clot:
a golden fleece moulds on a stalactite;
skeleton warriors waltz in the dark corners.

Atop and heavy, Liverpool tightens, glowers.
He disapproves. *I'll be driven out of town.*
A drill snaps down on our skulls.
We shatter like shells.

2.

Sometime after dark

I know that hurt
colliding as dust

                over bones,

the poor lady's beer-addled bones,

in the dark comes before

      the bee hive city squeeze,

in the street comes before

      avalanche of brick.

Thick blood
comes before

the fall.

My city is wearing costume jewellery tonight—
glittering and unreal.

A Red Moon

I break the top from the cathedral
and it comes,
                oozing steam,
cream,   champagne,
a thick cloud on the ground,

is a cake now, a castle, an island,
a ship, a table, pip in an apple, an eye,
an overweight seal on the edge of the tide.

It loves me I think,

heavy under sheets
            of water-clogged cloud.

The city is a man.
            He raises terraces, parks,
streetlight eyes,
to see moon simmer on paving skin.

He walks.
            I cling.
He wants to take me home
to sleep stretched over the shore,
            to fall,
                        shorting,
    hot and sweet—

to leave me surly
but settled in the street:

breath in the night, three stars,
            ice at toes, a haze
of streetlamp orange and fumes
and this road is a gate,
it seems, that leads
to the other side of town like an arrow
and burns—
                        the flames
standing up from yellow hyphens
that mark the tarmac,
joining its thinking into streets and suburbs.
Fire burns,   fire burns,

        in this skin,
        in a car engine,
        in the threshing blue of the sea—

across the town from here,
        sun leaps into deep plum distance
and a full-shadow midnight white
                    raze and cut of moon
on the well-lined multi-storey roof
where lamp lit eyes
blink now at bubbling rain-sky,
        fat-laden midriff-spinning,
        end of the ocean,
        end of an evening rain.

Thinking of love,
momentarily pass to you—

stood absent in shadow,
stood absent in the park,
stood absent in the dock—

or you absent in the cemetery
where a granite wall, smooth and shiny dark,
                                is a top hat
balanced on the edge of the quarry

—they took the sandstone
                from this furrow
spooned it north into brick and mortar—

mausoleums
stone angels:

                a spring
levels from the rock
pours its wetness over mulch and moss
of autumn passed
as night irradiates with moon,
statues,
        arms aloft,
catch unseen, the past:

a sailor sings calypso
        heard at the docks,
tail-coated gentleman
        is lost in fog,
and a child in a nightgown
        runs into town,
                cotton wet on thin legs,
                        she slips quick into

this cross-hatched night:
servant girl carries laundry,
butler waxes railings with shoeshine.
In a carriage without a driver
a thin black horse plumed and warm
draws a hearse of white bones
to the burial ground.

The light is hot.
The city is burning up
     with fires that have passed,
     or should have passed,
             but linger
                  gold at a touch.

     ~

Triangle shards
of glass in
     edgy water
          sap the light,
     threads of weeds
like stitches:
     these eyes
buckle on the reach
of stone, its push into
          itself
bobbing back from the air
into substance,

and across heavy roofs
naked
     with new rain

[8]

sky is tumbling,
bottoming up and over
                    colour
on colour—
                    a blast of
red through to blue.

A tap on my shoulder,
breath, bright face,
a crowd
a fray—
I keep the dead
deep and quiet
under stone:

a dancing slither
of hips and knees.

        ∼

The cathedral
bustles under a smear of sky,
clouded and marooned.

I force it home—
take the elegant thick
                    of cement and brick
and toss it
                    upended
out over the river
like a shot

and revealed
                    a hive of bones
that jiggle about maggot-like,
                    burrowing up and under
white cold
on white cold

and
back on the street in the under gloom haze
in the fat dark, ripe and blooming
night betrays
its own distinction
ebbing into black for a moment
then back into blue.

Night River

East to west, west to east,
wetness crawls

the promenade wall.
Oil and chemical, salt and tar:

the night is in my throat.

I consume distances
at the edge of the river,

three a.m., solitary
held only by the rain and the sky.

The wind's touch is courageous.

The stars are stags,
antlers pointed at each new shore

sailors discover
far from here, in some sunny waters.

I open to it like a mouth

and sense her shining
full height on the horizon,

as if the horizon is a ledge
she balances upon,

and hovering I rush to her,
her starriness, her electric pulses

that beckon, she widens:

I immerse myself in her thighs.
Her whiteness, her size.

I am her: the sea is a boat.
We ride until the dawn.

Seams of Dust

The pavement erupts and the past
—tail twitching—
rises from the cracks.

I lie face down on the road,
cars circling like lions.
A wolf howls on Church Street.

Two eyes,
yellow radar seeking scent.
Stay still. Keep calm.

Hear the ground break,
hear the ground break open.
Hold tight to the day,
the ends are streaming in the wind.

See the stars in the earth's belly shine.
See the stars in the earth's belly die.

Too much choking my throat.
Be silent now, be silent.

A flurry of ravens sweeps through the underpass,
talons reaching out for meat.
Do not encourage it. Do not speak.

There. It will pass back into the shadows.
Someone has turned the lights on.

It's done.
Take hold of my hand.

The Clock Tower

I see the right hand smile.
           A line
           from five across to nine
           turns to a curve.

Along unlit back streets
I am running for home.

In the shadows dust shines.
Bright things,
it seems are fading—
my watch, the window where
a family settle for the evening,
           shiny filament of an electric lamp—

all are thin
           faded by the burning of my eye
           by passing.

And the city loves me for it—
           wants my bones
           inside its bones,
seeking out
passages of self,
           the alleyways
           lanes:
      this puzzle of home.

Contradictions
are a dark alley
in a grey light,

      this messed up distilled light—

where the smile
on the clock face dwindles,
and the smile
on every fly poster
on the scaffolding fades
and every smile
on every advertisement
sinks back into the past,

a scar on a belly;
an organ removed.

The damage is a ghost.

        Do not burden it.
        Keep it close.

Do everything you can,
until battered round streets
to the river you go into the thick sludge,
until you are sleeping under
the heart of the river.

No answer though—
a certain kind of light.

Listen!   There
the memory of kindness
reaching into a night I can not touch.

Headlights

Litres of rain.
A consumption.
Enter the old weighed
net and block of buildings
—erode, erode,
the sandstone says.

Seven a.m. shadow.
Terrace window curtained shut;
blank canvas waiting for intention.
Her husband has died; she sees ghosts.
A kitchen lamp left on all night,
past fires flicker
like a lighthouse beacon,
brush on the window.

As the city calls out,
heads quiet
in before-day sleep,
open mouthed
wails slide out;
flat on feather,
sleeping bodies
quiver. Foghorn
on the river
and it's over.

Parkland

Skating through trees,
you could break your neck on the moon.

Like a paper doll you expand your body on the breeze,
shadow after shadow.

These versions of you hesitate, sit down,
climb trees, play Frisbee, give birth.

There is nobody else in the park but you,
reclining on benches, naked, smiling,

running between branches, distances,
mending ships' sails on the dilapidated bandstand—

you make rope in the avenues between cherry trees,
weave it round the pedestals of statues.

You wear a crinoline and row armoured carriers across the lake,
swans at your ankles like terriers.

You break your neck on the moon:

exercise horses on the sandy track looped around the edge of the park,
deliver laundry to old women in houses with broken windows.

You lie in the grasses in the small hills beside the streams,
touch yourself whilst looking at the sky.

You run naked in darkness across the open parkland,
starlight still wet on your back.

Andraste's Hair

In the woods they are burning her hair—
                              three of them.
They light it with a match
and she lets them,
she lets them burn her hair.

Watches the ends smoulder.
Watches the ends curl her curls,
curl up like leaves.

She lets them burn her hair.
There are long dark shadows
                    between trees
                    like corridors
blocked with boulders.

—The area is cordoned off—

She let them burn her hair.

—The area is cordoned off—

When the sun splits open

the gaps between trees

and the sun slices into the scene,

they see:

that she let them burn her hair.

        ∿

The light opens up the morning.

[18]

A plait laid out on the end of the bed
                              like a rope—
several metres long it hung there
swaying,
                   tied with a yellow bow.

It belongs to no one now—
lopped off at the nape of the neck.

The door is closed.

         ∾

Arms raised to hug the sun.
Woman,
                   eyes like sods,
ratchet-nosed, craggy—
hatchet arms creak and clank.

Lady,

sleeping under sunless light,

another sun gone,

reaching obedient: she dreams.

         ∾

From among the ashes,
from what had not burnt,
         gathered to a mass
of brown turf gathered
         her hair
and carried

—a cloud in her arms—
and carried
      to the river
      her hair
to spread in the warp of water.

The light smooth and silting.
The forest behind—
      remember
too much   too much
      dark cannot exist?
      The sun swings to the right.
She went left
      to the river,
      old dirt track,
stepping over grass,
hair taken down to depth.

In the forest they look for her.

Now,

she walks along the path by the river,
her hair in her hands
      to deliver
what had been taken
      to the river,
      to the water—
the smooth strand that curves its path
over the head of the hill.

Something subsides.
Something has passed.
Behind in the forest,
           in half dark heaving afternoon,

they claw at earth,
scratch around for a trace
                    and further
in the woods
search through evidence,
make lists of explanations,
make lists of reasons
for her absence.

The sun guides steps,
        footfalls—
        imprint on soil.

        ∾

It wasn't about who was listening.
If anyone was listening
        —to the song not the words—
speaking would mean silence
        —dead ears, dead ears—
but variation,
the pull and placing
in a line brimmed to full
        with evocation—
was almost love and almost listening.

Quiet response to quiet sound.

        ∾

A song heard in the forest days later,

burbled—

made a young boy cry.

Wrapped round trees,
stayed, not moving,

           just hung—

a stopping place.

We could meet
in the woods by the river,
stand eye to eye
in the stopping place
          and wait—
words curdling our bones
          to stone,
    be petrified

          in sound—
a single drum beat, one long groan.

While she walks
a path behind her concertinas,
each stride a fragile weight
that
      pushes up the earth,
turf over grass over turf.

Know how
it is now to be stone now,
to know how to finish.

Listen, she'll break you.

Will you follow?

The Fair

Local gods sit in judgement
                              selling jam
and the bonfire ready for the night's
                              display
is not on fire.
It squats. Pile of wood and paper.

A flickering animal eye wet and yellow
                 from deep
                              within
                              stacked wood
sees me.
Ceases.

An old woman
curves her bony hips
        and purrs slowly on
like a stalking cat.
Tongue on teeth in a dry mouth
hisses — as a girl,
like a thread between her legs,
        runs to hobble her.

A man
nabs the collar
of the girl before

she bobs
beneath
the stall —

as if under
thick translucent water.

Shadows contain
specks of light, random points of fine white.

Tent poles shake. A distant cloud
is pulling itself close.

Who hears it move?
Who hears the rain approaching?

    ~

Lantern-sky; pools of yellow after dark.
Each body still now, each body
around the wood pile waiting.
Outside fences, past the car park,
empty squares of dark field are
                        unspoken.

Fairy-lights and torches focus bright
                  upon wood.

Little breath. Much wide-eyed hope
        for crackling red
                    agitation.

The still evening air is hurt again.
Yellow lurches and orange claws.

Wait now. Wait for it.

No end to it. Keep the heavy wreck of it.
Keep the head smacking hot red body mash of it.

The circle in the circle
where children stand, muscles tense,

    ready to ache at it.

    Wait now. Wait for it. Wait.

Or snow

Later, houses know:
taxi on the avenue,

pearl windows,
far under.

My hand on wet glass
clears a porthole.

Women pasted white
against doorways,

their children
at their thighs.

Mermaid

She thinks about the sea,
about sailors alone at night,
about oysters,

clams, lichen on the bow
of the boat bidden beneath black cold
by the weight of sail and cargo.

His foreskin is smooth,
strange and cool.
Her tongue on the shaft
tastes the sea

—a memory
of seal skin,
her own fish scale,
her fins.

Working the Land

The field has no fences.

It is tilled
until it freezes
and the soil jams with ice.

Neat lines in the earth;
an anchoring of trees.

Carts of knotted wood
edge the furrows.

There is a sky

and it is heavy.

A blue fire,
the sort that bubbles
from a gas cooker,
burns in the furrows.

On either side of the horizon
are clouds of greying rain,
ambivalent and keen to smother.

The field has no fences.

And the light is muddy brown.

I only see in this light.

There are no fences.

We are ploughing.
Your face is in shadow.

[28]

Olwyn's Valley

1.

A steeple like a needle.
A dark wet wood
        and inside in
a crackle
of burning beeswax,
        tapestry cushions
mould with mildew.

The crypt underneath
is locked.

Back up on the hill—
the church from the distance,
squat, square and thick.
Black peat
        beneath
        a row of glandular trees.

A low moon
kept in a house of cloud
lets the light out slow
into a buckling valley
enormous and illumined
now with white.

The steeple forces
into the green moss,
sky, face first,
a strong arm round the neck,
threads it under
until neat and sharp
        it pools
in caverns
in the now blue dark.

2.

Carrying the edge of sunset
in the reflection of water,
the collusion:
red on spots in puddles
of purple where algae
gropes around the edge.
Bottle-nosed lichen
sniff like hunting dogs.
A man straddles a gate,
strides to the river,
reaches his cut hand
in to clean the wound,
so water runs red
to the sea,
—vein to vein.

3.

Stars in a storm
or jewels: the light from the sky
catches on each surface,
clears it, freshens its dark.
Lets the colour out to shine:
a shower of soft water.

4.

A house in the village where they are afraid of swimming;
where they fear water. The walls in the house

are rough to the touch. Run your hand,
it will catch on a jagged edge.

There is a table in the room.
It is also rough, made of oak.

On it are laid
the plates for dinner

though a staircase
that runs into the room

is empty
and the upstairs rooms

are empty
and the kitchen

is empty. The
family are by the sea
looking for their father, their son.

July

Weather-hurt and weary
she stands silenced—

gorse tongue
scratches her breath;

scent of smoke,
or the ghost of smoke,
dries in her lungs.

Remembering—
the sense of salt,
its purpose on skin.

Heat battens the day
to stone,
seals all edges into
a whole:
a monument of sun.

Body,

reclaiming

wet-solid heat

in the breast
under breasts.

Sharp lace
on nipples
       as sequins on
       the dress
       shift.

Eyes smart on
smoke,
       sticks
to nape,
             sweaty neck,
sticky skin
       and plucked brows
recovering
       light on
             shaved legs.

Night's growth
       of stubble
             stumbles in.
Skin stuck to skin
and sleeve stuck to skin.

Her fist on her collarbone
tests out a heartbeat,
        discovers it
thundering
under her nails.

Thickly close
it could climb out from her:
a heart birth.

Castle Hill

Surface

The summer has fallen off,
days turn to dust.

The hill battered with flames,
wind-rocked night-blasted,

burning in the dark in defence,
burning to be seen

naked on the horizon—
a thin seam of light.

A line of hands waving.
They are sinking

into the hill's heart,
deadened.

They force the night to bend.
Change direction, turn to dawn

and there are tears
and attempts to talk

tearing the hillside,
eating into its hide.

2.

Underneath

Born of peat bogs, mud pools,
their earth bodies rock,
sandy-featured granite-eyed;
they feast on minerals, taste salt
and metal—the substance of soil
tongued. Our eyes in the dark
like voles, yellow seeing
hazy outline of movement
curling around tight space
depth has given us, reduced
dimension and intimate
motion, the pulse of nothing,
a turning violent heart-rended
subtraction that leaves
us pawing at distances,
long claws tracking
passage back through caverns;
our hands sense
cool rock to act as guide. In the dark
we see with fingertips,
the journey—after and before—
relying on the twists
of sensation,
to take us home.

Tell me something of this

1.

A man, shuffling, shifty-eyed,
red coat cloaked, walking crab-like
underwater; rock pounded with rain.
Tell me about wetness, about sun,
clouds in the distance, the wind,
pole star burning white furnace hot,
early moon, mountains raised in ice,
new harvest of spires, town hall
clock face an oval pearl
untouchable submerged in night;
your bodies deep in layers of wool,
your hearts deep in layers of skin.
Tell me something of this, the balance
and skill of walking, the curved wealth
of each smile, the screams
squandered in your bellies
that fuel each stubborn stride.

You have been found, pin-pointed.
Light circles your stance in the street.
Look up—listen! Sparrow on an aerial,
a handprint in the brick, a date embossed
above the hardware shop, 1900.
Think about the things that never change.
Water charging from drains, doorframes,
chimneys, slate tiled tops, locks,
glass and more glass, all seeing,
your turning steps avoiding raindrops,
quick-stepping troughs and buttressed
by buildings' collegiate cover;
crammed over you they stare
benevolent but with the light behind
silhouetted against a blue sky.

~

I need the yawns and wails you hide
spread-fingered and embarrassed. Tell me?
Wet woods and weathered lovers
huddled beneath a black umbrella. Clasp
each other tight and watch the rain.
One day there may be no rain.
Imagine an end. An end of endings.
Think of how your arms will burn
over hollows when the other has gone.

Tell me something of this.

~

How your dreams fold round your sleep.
How the nights are tremulous
bracken edged moorlands.
How when you pour yourself into another,
something is shaken.
Windows blink like burnt irises
and although you smile when it's over,
buildings frown, whisper 'traitor'.

How you need cool confines to command
the heart you left at home. Rain.
Gravestones seep in rain. Turn grey,
erasing letters that read 'remembered'
and shored up by walls, reassured,
you form grief into dimensions,
streets, shops, blocks, byways,
barriers, blockades, walls. Turn left.

Turn right. Walk. Don't walk. Stop.
Look! Can you see? Peer harder.
There the horizon, the future,
a buzzing mist of grit
to grind into new mountains.

Tell me something of this.

How you hide scurrying to cover
the cracks in your thinking, the creaky
joinery that makes ourselves cohere.
I like the breaks, the bits between.
I'll make welcome,
feed and shelter what you can not carry.

～

We keep locked
entrances and turnings, all ways south.
Climb barriers, battle over garden walls,
cross patios and private lawns at night
when the street lamps electrify
and burn the new laid tarmac; you mutter
names of things in case
they break or fade away.
I've seen that happen, whole streets on fire.
Ambulances screeching into view to find a river,
a thick oozy blue seeping out of town
as flames grit teeth. Bite white heat,
then nothing but cold day.

~

But nobody sees it happen.
This is astounding. Nobody sees
the concrete bath blur senses
till touch is a grainy rough graze
and sight, a blackening of angles to grey.

Touch again—fearsome.
Yet empty each stroke—
a fraternising of pain with pleasure
and the compromise brings nothing.
No climax. No racking revelation.
Just rain smoothing down the light.

Whose pain? Who took it home?
Battling green oak trees fall burdened
with ciphers,
letters bundled to the ground
washed from newsprint spell
unspoken needs
in the back street puddles.

Peer in and see faces gleaming back
—the love-worn, the wasted—
caught in water, snapshots,
in the dark pools of town,
in the quiet corners.

2.

A wild cat curled in the tree's arms—

a child is sleeping;
cars coil round her dreaming
high on the moor.

The tree is on a roundabout
and to get there you have to cross the road,
find a way through traffic,
walk over the moor
to rest in the warmth of the new city

where each dimension
is well-thought
and possible,
where nothing is the same,
where the walls protect with difference.

This is the end of similarity,
of regularity, of always staying the same,
of dimension and restriction,
of repetition—

flat lines and spaces
taken down and packed away.

The tree is a breast.
It feeds its inhabitants
as they curl into the crooks
and kinks like small birds.

In her city
no one is a shadow,
nothing is taken at birth.

Can you
remember
     a shudder of skin in hot water
     or the fast ice of a hailstorm behind the station
that were not shouted
but possessed by a mind made of a skin?

      ∽

In the city on the moor
words bound from their mouths,
tumble each
other over
to fill the gaps
with explosions.

Below
they try so hard to sound the same
standardised and sure.
O so sure. So self-certain.
They enjoy their sentence.
They enjoy flapping
in self-made cages
like caught creatures.
      What fools!

I'll let them lie
as the lies build

cities that are lies.
Lie on lie on lie
cannot be true
but well-spoken
builds more lies.

~

Dreaming breaks into others dreams.
A tight corset
of desire
for things for things.
Dreams of ends
and revelations
that have been heard
seep up from the drains.

Who breathes with gills wide and open?

~

The girl comes to the city from the north.
It flickers like a broken star—
like a star that's been smashed with a hammer

and has crystallized,
each brick translucent;
now a window,
she can see the people
busying inside their houses with hot TV's gabble,
the warehouse pile of box on box of stuff.
Her city's warmth glows on the horizon.

And as she turns she sees the people are eating the city,
gnawing at bricks like rats at a bone.
Gobbling cornice like icing on a cake.

Their stomachs fill like balloons
or sacks, they carry
them in their hands,
wobble like pregnant sows.
They are sick with brick I think.

There is a corridor she loves.
It is in her old school.
A corridor not often used—
dusty, lined with wood and quiet.
She knows this is the way out.
But nobody asks her
and when she spoke
nobody heard.
She told a boy.

He runs there now,
clambers the gate, sound
of munching echoes in his ears.
Leaps the railings,
pounds over tarmac,
in through a window
and down to the corridor
which is silent and reserved
like a train waiting at a station.

She sees him slow in its confines

as if he runs on a treadmill.
Limbs circle in his joints.
He moves like a galloping horse
as the townspeople
chomp endlessly on mortar,
clogging their intestines
with cement.

      ~

Before they were split by last night's
revellers they spent the night in each other.
When she came he seemed to disappear,
to fall over a ravine,
to be behind a mirror looking at her eyes
                         —not being seen.

Wolf

Out along the lanes.
Out along the tracks.

Down to where the rain
is trapped in daisy heads.

Branches are dark now:
slithers of black.

She slips between
breaks of light,

an undertow,
an offering to fortune,

tumbles and scratches.

Fear flashlight,
searchlight, beacon.

See the spectrum wolf eyes see.

Pound fast, grey wolf,
carry yourself north

to thick tread of pine,
the reek of blood and oak.

Find a hollow of thorn and sleep.

Sky God Thunder

I have a necklace of blinking eyes around my neck.
The gleaming opulence of foul-mouthed city lights
shift across these fragile surfaces like tongues.

There: high and primary,
like the only thing that ever really did exist,
the moon, out for all to see—

the red of eyes,
thin lines stretched across the pupils like straw.

～

Turf wrapped overhead like a sky
of worms, and a far door in the dark:
the ends of a star
closed tight, it shimmers—
traces of light touching wood,
fat lines in thin navy muslin:
a woman door in a dress of darkness.
The tunnel is long and untouched by lies.
Its blueness is the way back into blue.

～

A striped lane walked towards the cairn,
rain holds my t-shirt to my chest many-handed.
The fields wept; we were wanted.
Lightning cuts through cloud,
a flare from a ship or flashlight in the underground.

In the dry crust of the hill
a cigarette butt dropped by another tourist
glows red, burns black.

August

Just the heat of her muscles'
rich red spasm.

Just the wild distances —
long grasses, horses.

Just the estuary mouth
to kiss at night-fall.

Just the city
ruled by wolves.

Just the dissolution
of brick.

Just the pleasure of rain
inside her

and the wet blue attitude of sky.

Flood

The rain tumbles on the living room roof.
I take off all my clothes

and walk beneath the window,
listen to the water colour and seal

gaps, cracks and troubled spaces
of this city, my home.

Streams and rivers I pull with me,
pull the depth of the sea

and estuary in the wake of my walk,
reel in the night and rain for you.

Come now, love, rest a while.
There is shelter in the flood.

Winter Dawn

The city is an envelope this morning
I slide into

and air—a fist of light.

The city is silent and gulls line the parapets
of traffic light lit gables.

The city falls about laughing.
Its sides split

aeons of dust in my mouth.

Reaching into the dawn,
my hands in his belly—

blood red sky, pale eyes.

          ∾

My lashes are twig-sharp.
Early-blue dawn.

The street beats
unbecalmed, smashed red.

It is felt time.
An instinct.

I can hear three voices
on the air—sunned voices,

crackling and orange—
burnt-edged noise.

Personify a lantern,
impersonate a lantern,

or a streetlamp
on an empty road
in February,

foggy and edged with
circles of rain.

Rain-naked

1.

Underwater, deep and bare,
in rain, in reflection,
sheared from a gaze
lie in wait for me—
in depth,
still, boneless,
in white water.

The fetch and carry of a winter's day
dreams itself weary of us and our demands—
of our weakening and waking
and falling

—these breakings
are molten spieling rain,

of bodies hooked
in the lake behind the avenue
of birch.

2.

The night is shut tight.
The day blinks.
The lino floor of my kitchen
is cold on our bare feet.
We are naked but these pelts.

The stone drinks in heat
as warmth tires,
falls home, earths,
thickens in sinew.

Our skins peel back to water
and we are blood creatures

pooling in the clouds,
reddening the day's bright cover,
puddling the moon.

Circle

Between summers and rainstorms
we sleep close and hot.

The night sky echoes
our shelter,

the roof
like all roofs—

the curve is a candle flame,

a drop of rain,
a shell

lengthening in our hands as we lengthen each other,

each gesture
coining gestures further from here,
further defined—

each delicate arc and spiral
part of our sky
that turns
above us as we turn upon each other.

We match the sky shape,

tree's leaf,
reel and furl

and the air
in the absence

between the walls.

On shore

Several hours of sunset
and the bells rang,

cockles
in a boiling pan,

out across the bay.

Inland, in a small room,
tired in her bed

she wraps warm legs
around her lover

and cries.

A Nocturnal Opera

1.

Setting.

Morning scold of dark
touches eyes shut dark

to see old dark waning.
All shades of dark,

frayed edge dark,
are now hollow head dark

in blue dark now a green dark a yellow dark
outside spectrum unseen dark to give it,

dark, properties of hot wet loose dark—
dwelling in corners

dark under the window
dark in my bed

dark in rooms without dark
window flat glass dark

in the street dark
in flowerbed dark

in gutter, wheels,
parked car dark

in passenger seat dark
church hall dust dark

post box clam dark
closed pub stain dark
rough fist dark
in flat upstairs dark

clambers across beds
downy dark

is brain and moist dark
is turned off dark
is shut down dark
is frontal lobe murmur dark
is neuron whispering dark
is lisping synapses dark
is slow blood dark
is darting dark
is semen dark

of small fry dark
is a jitter of dark
in dark
in dark
in dark
in slow blood.

I set off in the blue-black midnight,
flowers and shops closed and crowded with dark—

in soft warm blue,
barefoot, bra-less,

flung westward.
Day-sounds patter and fall,
recurrence, sameness, abstraction fall to earth

and are remade in the body of the dark,
floodlit, thick-heated night drags on;

thick with sleepers coiled in gluey dreams,
thick with smuggled children looking for homes,

thick with walkers crashing into poles,
thick with ends,

thick with slipwires,
thick with the day's remains.

This skin is a survivor
of too many nights swollen and slippery,

under the flow of a flurry of fingertips.
Touch is an answer to unasked questions.

Touch is a signal, settle, redress, undress.
Touch has many surfaces.

A mouth is a touch moving without destination
through night street's touch of air on a cheek.

The touch is parallel,
result of touch no touch without touch—

past textures gleam through sticky air,
touch faces with your open mouth,

touch fleeting presence with your presence—
touch the ends of days with the fresh touch of your mouth.

2.

Turning.

You lean on the alley wall,

hand on the wall, hand in my skirt.
The alley is dark, the stars lonely.

I come here at twilight
to give life to your mouth.

Brick grazes my shoulder.
The spark of the streetlamp on my pupil.

I am where the curve of your spine meets the night.
I am where the line of your arm crosses the dusk.

I am where the moon rises,
behind you a cool globe,

your face then part of the landscape,
your profile, moon geology—

your eyes are a tunnel between worlds.
'Meet me in the woods' you say and vanish

and I panic, scratching at the brickwork,
grain and grime in my nails,

opening gates and turning over plant pots,
looking into dustbins, disturbing cats.

A bedroom window lamp lights up
'Who's there?' cry voices out into the night.

I slip behind a tree and wait.

Dusk swells. Clouds congeal.
A black cat licks at my boots.

There is a shuffling on the horizon—
aircraft or gun fire.

The terraces are drunk
or dancing,

it's hard to tell.

The gardens are sprouting
thick-trunked oaks

rising.

The earth at the centre
cracks like eggshells.

The forest appears.
It has been dozing underneath the town—

opens up and stretches,
forms cavernous arches

over the houses, over the alleyways, over the moon—
until all light from the cosmos

wells under leaf,
wefts and weaves of leathery green,

a new roof, a new sky—no stars.

I reach along the garden wall,
find my way back down the street

by touch, finger on railing,
finger on lamp post.

They flicker on and off like blinking eyes.
Small pools of orange light

reflect the turrets of trees
that surround the school,

the nursery, the doctor's surgery,
my grandma's house, the bank.

And as I become accustomed to the gloom,
moonlight re-ignites—

a new breath after the shock,
and I can see monks in purple robes

processing past Woolworths,
and a grey wolf howls on the corner.

I can see a baby
swinging from a traffic light.

I can see a child
carrying an eye.

I can see a thin old man
with long hair

running—

his cheeks red,
his heart visible in his chest,
a hot coal in a hearth.

I can see stars piled high as old tyres.

I can see Jupiter's rings hooked on the church tower.

I can see the sun buried in the public gardens,
its red fuzz steaming from freshly dug soil

like steam from a horse's breath on a cold morning.

Circles conjure.

I can see a man with no clothes
covered in scratches.

He paws under the shadow of an oak
smitten with grasses and insects.

I see two lovers mime conversation.
The sun's death burnt out their lips.

They call softly, love by candlelight,
wallow in silence, abandon language.

I can see him slipping away
into a dark grove of sycamore.

Giant like beanstalks.
Giant like skyscrapers.

I follow, ridiculous,
a clown with over sized feet,

and enter the dark, sun-hurt, light-whipped.
Darkness smells of sweat.

It is a muscle. It carries time. It carries hurts.
But never breaks or suffers

—a light sparks—a last fallen star in the dark

revealing stark bark edges,
white and black like flaking skin,

then softens. Fire,
the last push of electricity,

spatters torches of heat along back streets
like snakes tongues.

The leaves sooth suddenness,
draw the shutter, pull in the ropes—

and the distant motorway is eaten alive
and the pylon in its compound chatters on

and stones of the wall
that run along

a track to the old farm
glow as if they are

wired by bulbs—
are a procession of candles.

I run towards the old dark
where the sentry tree

is naked; or more so
is an erection, a guardsman.

The stones glow as if they are coal.
They also are showing me their heart.

3.

Becoming.

In the forest, trees have no substance—
are octopus, flailing blue veined.

The wind raises an angry hand.
I follow.

Each branch is a nerve,
        heating and breaking,

carving and rending
        from fixed state to frenzy

and each hurt is a root
kneading mulch with knuckles

to form a woman—sap-bloody,
new born lost in the forest,

[64]

in a fairy tale—
in an old story.

I lift a weary head
from cotton-soft thorns,

eyes shiny and trembling
within blood and wood-born skin:

overheard on the breeze, trees sing—

'to kiss her taste wax leaf sweetness,

hold her to root her so sure,

plant her into darkness,

twist to one stem—
breasts, torso,

a pelvis to turn her—

she buds
and her hair is a halo.

Soil is a cover.
Night is a nest.

Her thigh's width weighs of wood.

Her eyes see centuries.
Her heart knows

rain and sun:

on the inside of her retina
the true angle of the moon.'

O this is green.

Green you move, green
        you so green—
        me under
green
        night so green
    is the green of grass,
green under spotlight,
                    green is mute.
Green wells of green,
            poured rain green
on river green,
            a dream of green seeps constant green
beneath grey green always green glanced twig green

new spring green—
O cut grass green.
O green field discipline.

I wake in the dark.
The forest is a hood.

Birds cackle: jackdaw gun gabble.
The cold space between my eyes is green and light.

The moon settles unseen into my skull,
it is warm in these thoughts.

I breathe beams—
pinpoint substance in darkness,

to reassure, to keep constant.
A passing shadow, owl laughter.

I have torn my breath
over leaves,

fallen over mulch dark,
scrambled over borders.

A cloud of air on my lips
taken by the cold.

I wait to return to bone
and journey into the sun's ebbing glue-red.

Breath is an eye—
it sees in time.

Hours trapped in the belly of the dark
tick unheard.

The moon bleeds on a star,
phallus hooked and shiny wet.

Night is a false end.
The sun is a lie.

Red light hungers over the dusk.
An appetite.

4.

Being.

Slow moving shadows lithe in the dark.

The tree absorbs the rain,
drinks the cold,

warms my thinking,
surrenders nothing—

is a patchwork of fibres
like panelling, like tiling,

lets no light in,
eats the light,

strangles the light—
is consistent,

is plentiful,
is absorbing.

The tree, like bone,
has a marrow—

marrow is all my thinking,

as thinking is tired and broken,
has no cohesion,

is swelling up,
is bloated,

is ugly—
is over important.

Thinking thinks too much of itself,
thinking is a red rich blood stain
clotted in my veins—

the tree can thin it with lightning and storm fire.

New ideas of colour,
storm thoughts—

ideas of bark,
an idea of green.

The ideas well and sooth,
are balmy, are oil.
They seep and settle.

Branches at an angle, a crescent moon.

Outside, above, ice forms on the bark skin walls.
I am inside my skin.

Your blood inside me like a system of stars and galaxies.

Your blood in my veins like axe marks on a tree stump.

The outside wells in my roots—
I drift, I sleep; wander through myself.

The nights are subtle, huge and bare.

They confide in me
all their hurried wind-felled dreaming,

the nightmare of dawn, of sun and season.

   5.

Ending

I bite my way clean
beyond fibres, beyond bark;

gnaw rat-toothed
at the guts

sap on my tongue,
the blood of a tree in my mouth.

I eat my own bones,
gnaw at my own hand—

jagged and hard-edged.
I taste of aniseed.

I cut at my tongue till it bleeds.

A scramble of insect legs over rock
as night tumbles towards dawn.

I eat my own heart.

When I have consumed myself
the mud is strewn with kindling.

I feel in the wind un-bodied
tissue thin and slide

into the gaps between tree trunk and stone.
It hurts to be free.